Leicestershire's Lost Railways
Neil Burgess

Melton Mowbray Station, 1951.

A rainy day at Syston Station on the Trent–Market Harborough line.

Text © Neil Burgess, 2018
First published in the United Kingdom, 2018,
by Stenlake Publishing Ltd.
www.stenlake.co.uk
ISBN 978-1-84033-759-4

The publishers regret that they cannot supply copies of any pictures featured in this book.

Printed by
Blissetts, E1 – 8 Shield Drive,
West Cross Industrial Park, Brentford, TW8 9EX

Picture Credits

The publishers would like to thank the following for contributing photographs:
John Alsop for the cover pictures, and pages 2–16, 19–42, 44–50 and 52–56;
Richard Stenlake for the pictures on pages 1, 17, 18, 43 and 51.

Closure Dates

This book lists dates when stations and lines were closed to regular scheduled passenger traffic. Readers need to recognise that sources vary in deciding closure dates, some giving the last day on which regular services operated, others the first day when closure was effected and no passenger traffic operated. Especially on lines with no regular Sunday service, this might yield a discrepancy of two days, depending on the method used.

In some cases, particularly before the mid 1960s, stations along closed lines might have been left substantially intact and periodically excursion trains might call to pick up or set down passengers. Where sources indicate that this happened it may be noted in the text, but it does not affect the official closure date.

Introduction

Leicestershire is the most southerly of the east midland counties and even in the twentieth century a great deal of it remains pastoral and agricultural in character. The city of Leicester was a Roman settlement and later an important centre during the middle ages, being well connected to the river network of the midlands. During the nineteenth century the industrial revolution took hold of the areas around Leicester and Loughborough and away towards the Trent at Burton, mainly through the development of coal mining and the manufacturing of bricks, tiles and pipes. Leicester and its environs also became a noted centre for knitwear and hosiery. Elsewhere the county retained its rural identity, though in the high ground of the Wolds ironstone was quarried during the late 1800s and early 1900s.

Leicestershire's railway network reflected this mix of geographical areas. Through routes, running north to south, connected the east midlands and Yorkshire to London, while east–west routes connected the growing west midlands to the eastern counties via Peterborough. These through routes, on the whole, are the lines which were among the earliest to be promoted and have survived into the present. In areas around centres like Coalville, Swadlincote and Ashby lines grew up to serve the industries which developed as the industrial revolution gathered pace. However, as these industries declined in the years following the Great War, the lines which served them also declined and, like the industries, eventually disappeared. In these areas, though not covered in this book (which concentrates on lines serving passengers), were to be found networks of goods and mineral lines serving collieries, factories and quarries, many of them built to standard gauge though a few narrow gauge networks also existed. These too have disappeared from the scene, though at least some of their engines have survived into preservation.

Leicestershire was very much part of the heartland of the Midland Railway, its main line from Derby to London including the Midland Counties line, originally promoted in the 1830s. However, the London & North Western Railway and the Great Northern Railway were also in evidence in the county, sometimes alone but also in co-operation with each other to challenge the Midland's entrenched position. The final major company in the county was the Great Central, descendant of the Manchester, Sheffield & Lincolnshire Railway and builder of the last main line in Britain before the twenty-first century, the splendid but ill-fated route to Marylebone.

Given the balance of companies in Leicestershire in the pre-Grouping era, it is interesting to see that the age of railway preservation has seen the revival of the Great Central, initially between Loughborough and Belgrave & Birstall, on the northern edge of Leicester, but hopefully in the near future to be extended northwards to Ruddington on the southern fringe of Nottingham. The London & North Western and Midland companies are also represented in the five-mile stretch of their joint line between Market Bosworth and Shenton, which operates under the title of the Battlefield Line. Only the Great Northern is unrepresented. Significantly, the role of industrial railways, particularly those associated with extractive industries, is celebrated in Rocks by Rail, formerly the Rutland Railway Museum, located on one of the former ironstone lines near Cottesmore.

For some years the county boasted a very singular piece of steam railway preservation in the form of the Cadeby Light Railway. This was the creation of the Reverend Edwin Richard 'Teddy' Boston, Rector of Cadeby with Sutton Cheyney near Market Bosworth, who constructed an 18" line around his rectory garden on which to run Pixie, a Bagnall saddle tank which he had obtained when the ironstone quarry in which it worked no longer needed it. Teddy Boston, long-standing friend of the Reverend Wilbert Awdry, 'creator and only-beggetter of Thomas the Tank Engine', died in April 1986, but for some years the railway was maintained by his widow, Audrey, in his memory. Sadly the line has now gone, but a bas-relief image of Pixie is included on the village's nameboard.

Included in this book are lines in the historic county of Rutland, which was incorporated into Leicestershire in the local government reorganisation of 1974 but which has since been accorded the status of a unitary authority.

Burton & Ashby Light Railway

Passenger service withdrawn   19 February 1927
Distance   11½ miles
Original owning company   Midland Railway

There were no stations in the traditional sense on this light railway; trams called at designated stopping places along the route, the line running between the main line stations at Burton and Swadlincote.

This section of the Midland Railway's empire was one of the more curious. Designated a light railway, it was in reality an electric tramway which for much of its length ran along public roads between Burton-on-Trent and Swadlincote in the same way that any other of its kind would; there was also a section of almost a mile between Sunnyside and High Street at Newhall which had its own reserved right of way across the fields.

The line's origins lay in demands for better transport in the growing south Derbyshire industrial area south of Burton around the beginning of the twentieth century. The Midland Railway was fearful that such a system would attract traffic away from its Swadlincote loop line, so in 1902 it applied for a Light Railway Order to construct the line. Once granted, work on the line began three years later and the first trams ran on 13 June 1906, operating on a gauge of 3' 6".

The tramway was a great success in its early years and became a well-established local institution. However, in the changed economic circumstances of the 1920s it was decided that the trams were no longer a practical alternative to the increasingly common motor bus and the line closed on 19 February 1927. Relics of the line survived for many years and the car sheds at Swadlincote became workshops for local collieries, eventually passing to the National Coal Board.

Harby – Bottesford – Newark *

Passenger service withdrawn   see text
Distance   15½ miles
Original owning company   Great Northern and London & North Western railways (south of Bottesford); Great Northern Railway (Bottesford – Newark)

Station closed	Date of closure
Redmile **	7 December 1953

* The closed station on this line that was in Nottinghamshire was Cotham.
** Closed between 15 January and 19 March 1951.

Although the London & North Western and Great Northern railways were often rivals over their parts in the west and east coast main lines, they made an alliance against a common adversary in Leicestershire and Nottinghamshire when faced with the early dominance of the Midland Railway. The London & North Western wanted to gain access to the east midlands and did so by allying itself to the Great Northern over a long and straggling line running through some very sparsely populated uplands in Northamptonshire and Leicestershire from Northampton, through Market Harborough and Melton Mowbray to the Great Northern's Nottingham – Grantham line at Saxondale Junction. From there London & North Western trains exercised running powers over the Great Northern into Nottingham London Road Low Level station and to a London & North Western goods depot in Manvers Street.

The line opened in sections, the one from Newark to Marefield Junction, south of John O' Gaunt in Leicestershire, being authorised in 1872 and the joint line two years later. Despite its outlay, the London & North Western never made a major inroad into the Nottinghamshire coalfield and the thinly populated Leicestershire uplands yielded only stone traffic, while iron ore was quarried around Eastwell and Waltham-on-the-Wolds, which supported a small network of mineral lines diverging from the 'main' joint line at Harby.

Passenger receipts were also sparse and this traffic north of Bottesford ceased in the first weeks of the Second World War. Passenger traffic ceased completely in 1953 and goods in 1962.

A surprising amount of the line still exists, particularly in Leicestershire, the bridges, viaducts and stations remaining half a century after closure.

Leicester – Burton on Trent

Passenger service withdrawn	7 September 1964	*Stations closed*	*Date of closure*
Distance	31 miles	Ashby-de-la-Zouche *****	7 September 1964
Original owning company	Midland Railway	Moira	7 September 1964
		Gresley	7 September 1964

Stations closed	*Date of closure*
Kirby Muxloe	7 September 1964
Desford (first station) *	27 March 1848
Desford (second station)	7 September 1964
Bagworth (first station)	27 March 1848
Bagworth & Ellistown **	7 September 1964
Bardon Hill ***	12 May 1952
Coalville Town ****	7 September 1964
Swannington	18 June 1951

* Originally named Desford Lane, renamed by 26 April 1833.
** Originally named Bagworth (second station) until 1 October 1894.
*** Originally named Ashby Road until 1 January 1847; closed between 1 March and 1 September 1849.
**** Originally named Long Lane until 27 March 1848, then named Coalville until 2 June 1924.
***** Originally named Ashby until 13 July 1925.

Kirby Muxloe Station, *c.* 1910

Bardon Hill Station, July 1952.

This 31-mile line was built by the Midland Railway to tap the heartland of the small but locally significant Leicestershire coalfield. It was opened throughout on 1 August 1849 and connected the main lines of two of the three companies which amalgamated in 1844 to form the Midland. At its northern end the line ran into Burton-on-Trent, on the former Birmingham & Derby Junction Railway, while at the Leicester end it connected to the route of the Midland Counties Railway. In between it served the small towns and colliery communities of Gresley, Moira, Swannington, Coalville and Bagworth and lined up to a number of existing lines, including the Midland's oldest constituent, the Leicester & Swannington.

Coalville Station.

Midland Railway station, Coalville

LEICESTER – BURTON ON TRENT

The station is to the left of the footbridge in this view of Coalville's High Street.

The area has been home to a number of canals, also built to carry coal, and as the railway waxed in its fortunes, the canals waned. Over the latter years of the nineteenth century larger collieries were opened and Coalville became not only a centre for the coalfield but also the third town in the county by population. After the Great War coal began a long slow decline and inevitably the fortunes of the railways which so depended on it declined also.

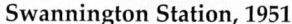
Swannington Station, 1951.

Moira Station.

As with other lines in this part of Leicestershire, train services were also affected after 1918 by the growth of buses and road transport generally. Passenger services were withdrawn in September 1964 and coal traffic continued into the 1970s, after which the line was 'mothballed' pending a decision on its future. Around 2009 there were proposals to reinstate at least part of the route for passenger traffic, while occasional workings of aggregates have occurred on occasions. At the time of writing, however, nothing of long-term import has been decided.

Leicester – Rugby

Passenger service withdrawn		1 January 1962
Distance		20 miles
Original owning company		Midland Counties Railway

Station closed	Date of closure
Wigston South *	1 January 1962
Countesthorpe	1 January 1962
Broughton Astley **	1 January 1962
Ullesthorpe ***	1 January 1962

* Originally named Wigston until 1 October 1868.

** Originally named Broughton until 1 July 1845; renamed Broughton Astley until 1 October 1870, then named Broughton again until reverting back to Broughton Astley on 15 September 1879.

*** Originally named Ullesthorpe until 1 May 1879, then Ullesthorpe for Lutterworth until 1 August 1897, then Ullesthorpe & Lutterworth until reverting to Ullesthrope on 1 February 1930.

Wigston South Station, 1951

Broughton Astley.

The Midland Counties Railway was one of the pioneering lines in the midlands, being originally authorised by Parliament in the mid 1830s at the dawn of the age of steam railways. It opened between Trent and Leicester in May 1840, a twenty-mile extension southwards to Rugby being opened from 1 July in the same year in order to make a junction with the London & Birmingham line. In due course the Midland Counties became a main constituent of the Midland Railway in 1844 and the London & Birmingham became a main constituent of the London & North Western Railway in 1846.

Ullesthorpe Station.

The Leicester – Rugby line was important as a means of connecting the Midland network to London; but in 1857 the Midland opened a new connection from Bedford to Hitchin on the Great Northern Railway, which afforded access to London with the added advantage that traffic to and from the east midlands ran for a greater distance over the Midland's own metals. Seven years later a direct link between Leicester and Birmingham over the London & North Western via Hinckley further reduced the significance of the Rugby line, which became very much a secondary route. It continued a leisurely existence well into the twentieth century, passenger and goods services being withdrawn from the first day of 1962 south of Wigston North Junction. There was later a possibility of reopening the line as a connection between the west coast main line and the east midlands, but by this time parts of the trackbed had been built upon and the idea was abandoned.

Leicester Belgrave Road – Marefield Junction

Passenger service withdrawn	7 December 1953 [but see below]	*Station closed*	*Date of closure*
Distance	10 ¼ miles	Thurnby & Scraptoft	7 December 1953
Original owning company	Midland Counties Railway	Ingarsby *	8 October 1962
		Lowesby *	8 October 1962

Station closed	*Date of closure*
Leicester Belgrave Road	7 December 1953
Humberstone	7 December 1953

* Spelled 'Ingersby' until 25 September 1939 and 'Loseby' until December 1916 respectively.

Leicester Belgrave Road Station.

Leicester Belgrave Road Station, May 1953.

This railway, although directly connected to the London & North Western and Great Northern joint line at Marefield Junction, was the sole property of the Great Northern, giving Leicester a station belonging to a third company in addition to the Midland and the Great Central.

Leicester Belgrave Road, September 1946.

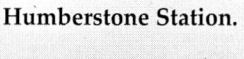
Humberstone Station.

The line was opened for goods traffic into the terminus at Belgrave Road in May 1882 and to passengers on 1 January 1883. However, even before the opening a sign of things to come was provided by the running of the first excursion service to the Great Northern's principal resort on the Lincolnshire coast at Skegness, which took place on 2 October 1882. Indeed, for many people going to Skegness was the main reason for using Belgrave Road, an impressive station which always seemed to have an abundance of space in relation to the traffic handled. The Great Northern provided trains onto the joint line and also a service to Peterborough, though this ceased from 1 April 1916 as a war economy and was never reinstated.

Lowesby Station

Belgrave Road, Humberstone and Thurnby & Scraptoft closed to regular passenger traffic from 7 December 1953, though until 29 April 1957 an unadvertised workmen's service to and from John O' Gaunt stopped at them. After 1953 Belgrave Road was used to store sets of carriages used on summer weekends for excursions to the Lincolnshire coast and this continued until these last passenger workings were withdrawn from 9 September 1962. Goods facilities lingered on until 14 December 1964, after which the entire site was cleared and redeveloped.

Leicester West Bridge – Desford

Passenger service withdrawn	24 September 1928
Distance	6 ½ miles
Original owning company	Leicester & Swannington Railway

Station closed	Date of closure
Leicester West Bridge (first station) *	13 March 1893
Leicester West Bridge (second station)	24 September 1928
Glenfield (first station)	1875
Glenfield (second station)	24 September 1928
Ratby (first station) *	1873
Ratby (second station)	24 September 1928
Desford (first station) *	27 March 1848

* Respectively, originally named Leicester, Ratby Lane and Desford Lane until 26 April 1833.

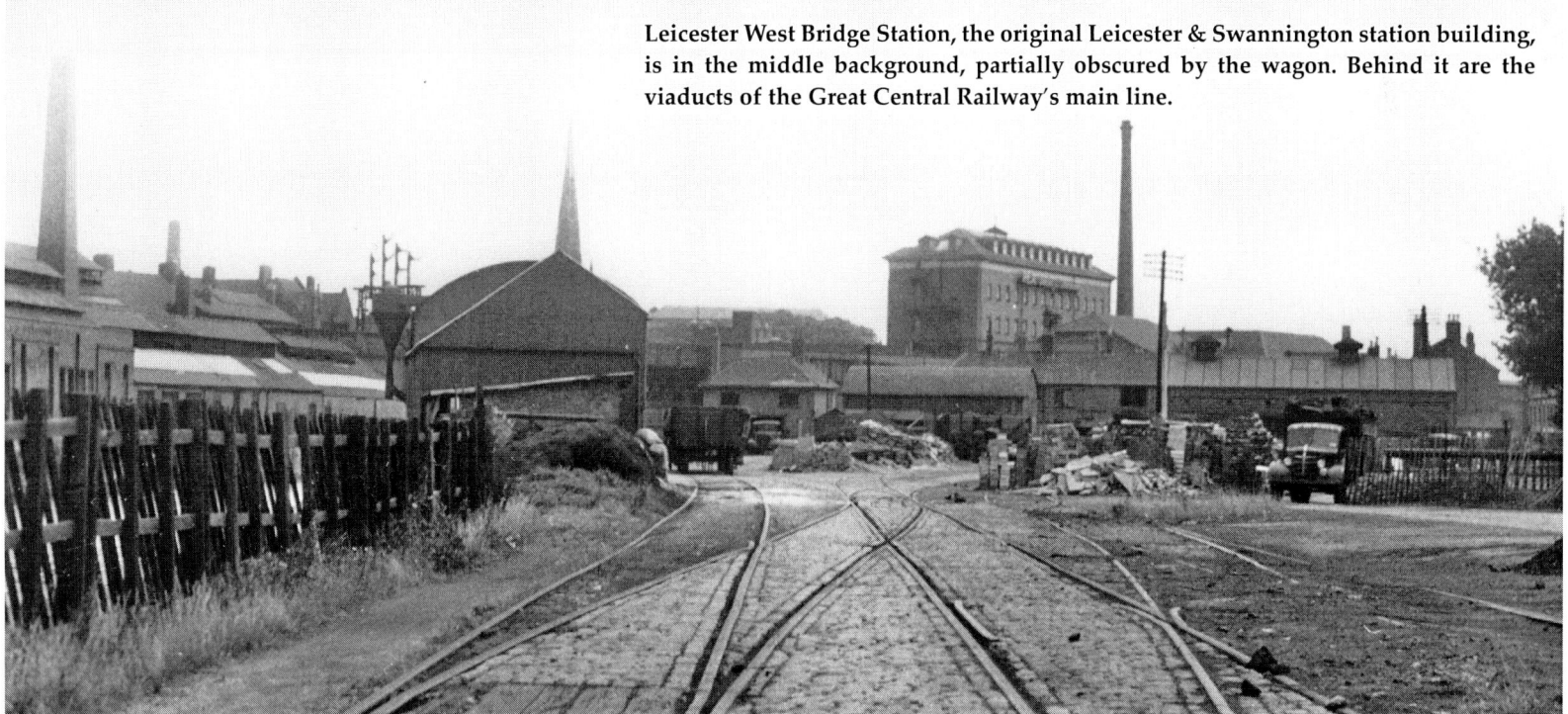

Leicester West Bridge Station, the original Leicester & Swannington station building, is in the middle background, partially obscured by the wagon. Behind it are the viaducts of the Great Central Railway's main line.

The Leicester & Swannington was the pioneer steam-operated railway in Leicestershire, built to carry coal from the coalfield to the River Soar in Leicester. Authorised by Act of Parliament in 1830, the same year as the Liverpool & Manchester, and opened in 1832, it was absorbed by the Midland Railway in 1847, making it that company's oldest constituent.

Glenfield Station.

The line was constructed over fairly easy country, though it was necessary to tunnel under Glenfield hill, just outside of Leicester, by a 1,796-yard earthwork which in later years severely restricted the locomotives which could be used on the line due to its narrow bore. The route's total length was sixteen miles, though only the section to Long Lane in Coalville carried passengers. When the Midland Railway took it over in 1847, a two-mile section near to Bagworth, which included an inclined plane at 1 in 29, was replaced by a new section of line. The Midland opened its Leicester to Burton line in the following year and this took over the Leicester & Swannington route between Coalville and Desford, the passenger service on the line being operated to and from Burton.

Ratby Station, July 1952.

In its independent days, passenger carriages were conveyed in coal trains and there were no stations as such, only recognised stopping-places, generally where the railway crossed a public road. Tickets were often sold from local inns, much as stagecoach tickets had been and would-be passengers simply hailed the train as it drew near. It was at one of these stopping places, near the Stag & Castle Inn in Thornton Lane, that the engine Samson was reputedly in collision with a cart, as a result of which the engine was fitted with a 'steam trumpet' or whistle: the first appearance of such a universal feature of subsequent engines. Recent history has cast doubt on this tale, though collisions between trains and road-users, the latter no doubt believing that they could get across the line in time or else failing to see the train altogether, were common enough then and since. During the 1970s some of the rudimentary stations along the line were rebuilt and the line continued to carry passengers until competition from motor buses took its toll and the service was withdrawn in 1928. Goods traffic continued to West Bridge until 4 April 1966, 134 years after the original opening, and thus vanished Leicester's link with the pioneering days of steam powered public railways.

Loughborough – Rugby: The Great Central Main Line *

Passenger service withdrawn	4 September 1967
Distance	29 ¾ miles
Original owning company	Manchester, Sheffield & Lincolnshire Railway (Great Central Railway from 1899)

Station closed	Date of closure
Loughborough Central **	5 May 1969
Quorn & Woodhouse **	4 March 1963
Rothley **	4 March 1963
Belgrave & Birstall **	4 March 1963
Leicester Central	5 May 1969
Whetstone	4 March 1963
Ashby Magna	5 May 1969
Lutterworth	5 May 1969

* The closed station on this line that was in Northamptonshire was Rugby Central.

** The line between Loughborough and Belgrave & Birstall was reopened in stages after 23 March 1974 (Rothley had to wait until 3 January 1976) by the Great Central Railway Preservation Society. The original stations were reopened except for Belgrave & Birstall, a new terminus, named Leicester North, being built just south of the original station site and opened on 3 July 1991.

Loughborough Central Station.

Quorn & Woodhouse Station, November 1965.

The Manchester, Sheffield & Lincolnshire Railway was, until the last decade of the nineteenth century, a provincial railway company concentrating its activities in the areas named in its title. During the 1890s it succeeded in transforming itself into a major trunk route from London to the north of England by the building of its London Extension, the last great main-line construction project before the Channel Tunnel rail link.

Rothley Station.

The story of the upper end of the London Extension has been related in *Derbyshire's Lost Railways* and in *Nottinghamshire's Lost Railways*. The line was opened on 15 March 1899, by which time the Manchester, Sheffield & Lincolnshire had become the Great Central Railway and gave both Loughborough and Leicester a third station each and a new route to London to compete with the Midland. In Leicester the Great Central strode across the city on a succession of viaducts and the station itself was a good example of the London Extension's predilection for a broad central platform approached from road level by steps.

Leicester Central Station.

109 Central Station, Leicester

Though the London Extension was a magnificent piece of engineering, the Great Central realised that it would have to work hard to capture traffic from the well-established Midland route. The Midland in the 1890s had to cope with the consequences of its own success, which saw traffic expanding beyond what the line could accommodate, so it might be argued that any loss of traffic to the newcomer might even have helped the Midland by reducing pressure on resources. The Great Central for its part determined to provide a service of fast, efficient expresses to and from London, lightly loaded and well within the capacity of a single engine. In this it was modestly successful, but its expresses contrasted with the long-distance all-stations stopping services over the route which could take hours to complete their journeys.

Leicester Central Station.

The London Extension passed to the LNER in 1923 and its new owners did their best to develop it as an alternative route to the midlands and Yorkshire to the East Coast main line. British Railways seem to have found it an inconvenience in some respects, passing it from Eastern Region to London Midland Region control in the 1950s. It was run down during the late 1950s, lost many of its intermediate stations in 1963 and closed entirely in 1967, though a passenger service from Rugby continued for a further two years, stopping short of Nottingham Victoria at Arkwright Street, close to the football grounds.

Great Western Railway locomotive No. 3056 *Wilkinson* with a train for Oxford, piloted by a Great Central locomotive at Leicester Central Station.

There has been much controversy about the wisdom of closing the line, critics pointing to its construction to European loading gauge which could, with the Channel Tunnel, have provided precisely the rapid access from France to northern England that Watkin envisaged. Others have argued that at the time the line was an expensive duplication of existing routes and that it is too easy to be wise after the event.

Lutterworth Station, August 1951,

Whatever the truth of these positions, others were determined that they would do something to preserve at least a part of the London Extension rather than just bemoan its demise. The Great Central Railway Preservation Society succeeded in re-opening the line southwards from Loughborough to Belgrave & Birstall from 1974 and the acquisition of the retained line northwards to Ruddington means that it will soon be possible to travel again from the outer fringes of Nottingham to the edge of Leicester by Great Central.

Loughborough – Shackerstone

Passenger service withdrawn	13 April 1931
Distance	16 ¼ miles
Original owning company	Charnwood Forest Railway

Station closed	Date of closure
Loughborough Derby Road	13 April 1931
Snell's Nook Halt	13 April 1931
Shepshed *	13 April 1931
Grace Dieu Halt	13 April 1931
Thringstone Halt	13 April 1931
Whitwick	13 April 1931
Coalville East **	13 April 1931
Hugglescote	13 April 1931
Heather & Ibstock ***	13 April 1931
Shackerstone	13 April 1931

* Originally named Sheepshed until May 1888.
** Named Coalville (L&NW) from 1 May 1905 to May 1910 when it was renamed Colville (LNW). Reverted to its original name of Coalville East on 2 June 1924. **
*** Originally named Heather until 1 September 1894.

Loughborough Derby Road Station, July 1951.

Shepshed Station, *c.* 1905.

The Charnwood Forest Railway was a notionally independent undertaking created to tap the coalfield traffic on the outskirts of Loughborough and Coalville in the upland area of Charnwood Forest, running southwards to join the Ashby & Nuneaton joint line at Shackerstone. Authorised by an Act of 16 July 1874, construction began in 1881 and the line opened on 14 April 1883. The London & North Western subscribed one third of the shares and undertook to work the line from the outset for half the receipts. The independent company fared badly and was placed in receivership after being declared bankrupt in 1885. It remained in the receiver's hands until 1909, but paid no dividend on its ordinary shares throughout its existence.

Whitwick Station, May 1965.

Hugglescote Station, May 1965.

As with the Ashby & Nuneaton, the Charnwood Forest, known locally as the 'Bluebell line', carried a good deal of coal traffic but relatively few passengers. The London & North Western tried operations with a steam rail car in the early years and halts were opened from 1 April 1907 at Thringstone, Grace Dieu and Snell's Nook, but these did little to alter the realities of the rural areas through which most of the line passed. Bus competition in the years after 1918 took its toll and scheduled passenger services ended on the same day as those on the Ashby & Nuneaton in April 1931. Excursion traffic continued to use the stations into the 1950s, but ceased in 1951. Most goods services ended on 7 October 1963, trains to Shepshed quarry surviving until 12 December.

Nottingham – Melton Mowbray *

Passenger service withdrawn	29 April 1967	*Station closed*	*Date of closure*
Distance	18 ¼ miles	Old Dalby	18 April 1966
Original owning company	Midland Railway	Grimston	4 February 1957

* Closed stations on this line that were in Nottinghamshire were Edwalton, Plumtree, Widmerpool and Upper Broughton

Grimston Station.

The Midland Railway was one of the earliest companies to operate in the east midlands and from its early days operated lines serving the major towns and cities in the region. Not surprisingly these lines tended to be constructed between adjacent centres of population, so places like Chesterfield, Derby, Nottingham, Loughborough, Leicester and Market Harborough were on the original north–south axes of its system. In due course, during the 1860s, this route was developed by the company's London extension and today is the route taken by trains from Derby and Nottingham to the capital.

As described in *Nottinghamshire's Lost Railways*, one of the problems faced by railways in the latter part of the nineteenth century was that their facilities and routes were regularly becoming congested as traffic grew beyond the expectations of the original promoters. To alleviate congestion at Trent, the junction between the Erewash Valley line and the line from Nottingham to London, a new line was built from Nottingham to Melton Mowbray where trains for London could be routed through Oakham and Manton, rejoining the original London line at Glendon South Junction.

As a main route the line was a great advantage, but the predominantly rural area through which it passed offered little originating traffic, either passenger or goods. The intermediate stations between Melton and Nottingham closed as early as the 1940s, though Old Dalby continued to be served by stopping passenger services until 1966. Under the Beeching Report of 1963 the northern section between Nottingham and Melton was closed in 1967, though trains still continue to use the route south of there. The section in Leicestershire found a new use as the test track for the experimental rail testing centre at Derby. Over the years the ill-fated Advanced Passenger Train [APT] and its successor, the Virgin Pendolino, have been tested there; one of the most spectacular tests was the staged collision of a Sulzer diesel, no. 46009, pulling a three-coach train, with a nuclear flask on 17 July 1984.

Overseal – Nuneaton

Passenger service withdrawn — 13th April 1931
Distance — 17 ¼ miles [Donisthorpe – Nuneaton]
Original owning company — London & North Western and Midland Joint Railway (aka Ashby & Nuneaton Joint)

Station closed	Date of closure
Overseal & Moira *	1 July 1890
Donisthorpe	13 April 1931
Measham	13 April 1931
Snarestone	13 April 1931
Shackerstone	13 April 1931
Market Bosworth	13 April 1931
Shenton	13 April 1931
Stoke Golding	13 April 1931
Higham-on-the-Hill	13 April 1931

* Station closed when the new Moira Station was built further east on the Burton–Ashby line.

Overseal & Moira Station, *c.* 1905.

Measham Station, *c.* 1910.

This was a line intended to serve part of the Leicestershire coalfield which managed to preserve a remarkably rural character throughout its existence. The origins of the line lay with the Midland Railway which in 1846 had planned a route all but identical to that which was eventually built almost three decades later, but the acquisition of the Leicester & Swannington line gave the Midland an alternative path into the coalfield and the powers were allowed to lapse. During the early 1860s the London & North Western sought access to the coalfield and intended to do so by making use of its Nuneaton to Wigston line. This in turn prompted the Midland to revisit its earlier plans and at one stage it looked like two lines might be promoted. The common-sense solution was a joint line, eventually opened to goods in August 1873 and passengers from 1 September in the same year. An extension from Stoke Golding to Hinckley was constructed but never opened for traffic, the track being lifted around 1900.

Shenton Station.

The Ashby & Nuneaton joint line, as it became known, enjoyed a considerable volume of traffic, mainly coal, but relatively few passengers. Nevertheless some of the stations were very impressive, not least Shackerstone, which was adjacent to Gopsall Hall and on at least one occasion seeing royalty alight. After the Great War the LMS found that even the relatively modest passenger traffic dwindled further in the face of competition from motor buses and withdrew the service in April 1931. Goods traffic survived until 1964, the facilities at Market Bosworth lingering on for a further four years.

Stoke Golding, May 1951.

This, though, was not the end of the Ashby & Nuneaton Joint. In 1969 a group set up a depot for preserved locomotives and rolling stock at Market Bosworth, moving to Shackerstone the following year when their first engine arrived. Progress was slow, but in 1992 the line ran as far as Shenton, almost five miles. Since then the Battlefield Line (which passes over the site of the Battle of Bosworth) has become firmly established as one of the smaller heritage lines in Britain.

Pear Tree & Normanton – Ashby-de-la-Zouch, including the Melbourne Military Railway *

Passenger service withdrawn	22 September 1930 (see text)	*Station closed*	*Date of closure*
Distance	14¾ miles (Pear Tree–Ashby; 16¼ miles from Derby to Ashby)	Ashby-de-la-Zouch ***	7 September 1964
Original owning company	Midland Railway		

* Closed stations on this line that were in Derbyshire were Chellaston & Swarkstone and Melbourne.
** Originally named Tonge until 1 May 1897.
*** Originally named Ashby until 13 July 1925.

Station closed	*Date of closure*
Tonge & Breedon **	22 September 1930
Worthington	22 September 1930

Tonge & Breedon Station, April 1952.

As recounted in *Derbyshire's Lost Railways*, the Midland line between Pear Tree & Normanton, on the main line from Derby to Birmingham through Burton-on-Trent, to Ashby-de-la-Zouch on the Leicester–Burton line, had a long and involved history. The section between Melbourne and Ashby was built as a 4' 2" gauge horse-worked tramway linking Cloud Hill lime works at Breedon to the Ashby canal, which had originally opened in April 1799. The Midland, aiming to tap into lucrative quarry traffic, acquired the tramway, converted it to a standard-gauge locomotive worked railway and extended it to Pear Tree, the whole route opening on 1 September 1868.

Worthington Station, October 1949.

It appears that passenger receipts were never very lucrative and fell even more with the advent of motor buses after the Great War. With the Great Depression after 1929 things looked worse and passenger services ceased on 22 September 1930.

Ashby-de-la-Zouch Station.

In 1939 another world war created an urgent demand for military rail transport and with it men capable of operating the railways in combat areas. To supplement the work done by the Longmoor Military Railway, the Royal Engineers took over the Ashby line for the duration of the war as a 'second Longmoor', the line becoming No. 2 Railway Training Centre, Melbourne, on 19 November 1939. The army maintained the goods service along the line, at the same time dramatically increasing facilities to cope with supplies and material assembled for campaigns throughout the conflict. The soldiers also constructed a series of prefabricated bridges along the route as practice for similar activities in theatres of war. After the United States entered the war in December 1941, American military railwaymen also used the line for training. After D-Day the military railway units also moved overseas to repair and maintain the railways in the wake of the allied advance into Germany. From 1 January 1945, the LMS resumed full control of the line.

The line continued as a through route until 1955, when the southern section into Ashby was closed. Tonge & Breedon closed to goods in 1959, Worthington in 1964 and Chellaston & Swarkestone in 1966. The final section of the line operated from Lount colliery to supply coal to Drakelow power station until 1968, after which the line was operated as an elongated siding from Worthington Junction to allow movement of occasional loads of limestone. Final closure came on 21 May 1980.

Saxondale Junction – Market Harborough *

Passenger service withdrawn	7 December 1953
Distance	38 miles
Original owning company	Great Northern and London & North Western railways (jointly)

Station closed	Date of closure
Harby & Stathern **	7 December 1953
Long Clawson & Hose ***	7 December 1953
Scalford	7 December 1953
Melton Mowbray ****	7 December 1953
Great Dalby	7 December 1953
John O' Gaunt *****	7 December 1953
Tilton	7 December 1953
East Norton *****	7 December 1953

Station closed	Date of closure
Hallaton *****	7 December 1953
Market Harborough (LNWR)	14 September 1884

* Closed stations on this line that were in Nottinghamshire were Bingham Road and Barnston.
** Originally named Stathern until 1 November 1879.
*** Originally named Long Clawson until 30 December 1884.
**** Sometimes described as Melton Mowbray North after the Grouping, though the name does not seem to have been official; the LMS renamed the former Midland station 'South' in 1923.
***** Closure to advertised services; see text.
  Originally named Burrow & Twyford until 2 July 1883.
  Replaced by the present LNWR and Midland joint station.

This line, along with Harby – Bottesford – Newark, was part of the Great Northern and London & North Western joint line network. See page 4 for the history of the network.

Harby and Stathern Station

John O' Gaunt Station, June 1949.

Tilton Station, May 1952.

East Norton Station, c. 1900.

Hallaton Station, October 1951.

A spur for Leicester – Peterborough traffic left the line at Hallaton Junction, just south of Hallaton Station. From there it ran 3¼ miles to Drayton Junction on the LNWR Market Harborough – Peterborough line. There was a single station on the spur at Medbourne, which opened in July 1883 and closed in April 1916 as a wartime economy.

Swadlincote Loop Line

Passenger service withdrawn	6 October 1947	*Station closed*	*Date of closure*
Distance	7¾ miles	Swadlincote [first station] **	1 May 1883
Original owning company	Midland Railway	Swadlincote [second station]	6 October 1947

Station closed	*Date of closure*
Woodville [first station] *	1 May 1883
Woodville [second station]	6 October 1947

* Originally named Wooden Box until 1 October 1868.
** Closed between October 1853 and 1 June 1864.

What became known as the Swadlingcote Loop began as two separate lines which were later joined together to form a through route. The area around Swadlincote and Woodville developed through the middle of the nineteenth century as a centre of coal mining along with brick, pipe and tile making. Swadlincote was the principal centre of population and from 1848 a line off the Burton–Ashby route was built to serve it, opening from 1 July 1851. Later another branch was built towards Woodville, then known as Wooden Box, which opened from 1 April 1859. From 12 April 1880 a new section of line joining the two was opened for goods, passenger traffic following from 1 May 1883.

The line conveyed a high volume of goods traffic and passenger receipts were always secondary. As with other lines in the populous industrial areas, motor bus competition took its toll in the inter-war years and the service was lost from October 1947. The stations remained intact and continued to be used for excursion traffic, especially during the summer months, but after 1962 this ceased and the stations were finally demolished. Most goods traffic ceased from 1964 but the connection to Cadley Colliery remained in use until the 1980s.

Blaby Station.

Stations closed on lines still open to passengers: Leicester – Nuneaton

Original owning company	Midland Railway
Stations closed	*Date of closure*
Wigston Glen Parva *	4 March 1968
Blaby	4 March 1968
Croft	4 March 1968
Elmesthorpe	4 March 1968

* Originally named Glen Parva until September 1887.

Elmesthorpe Station.

Leicester – Peterborough *

Original owning company — Midland Counties Railway

Stations closed	Date of closure
Humberstone Road	4 March 1968
Syston **	4 March 1968
Rearsby	2 April 1951
Brooksby	3 July 1961
Frisby	3 July 1961
Asfordby ***	2 April 1951
Saxby (first station)	28 August 1892
Saxby (second station)	6 February 1961
Whissendine ****	3 October 1955
Ashwell	6 June 1966
Manton *****	6 June 1966

* Closed stations on this line that were in Northamptonshire were Helpston and Walton. Closed stations in Rutland were Luffenham, Ketton & Collyweston and Uffington & Barnack.
** Reopened as a new station on 28 May 1994.
*** Originally Kirby until 1 December 1857 and then Asfordby (late Kirby) until 1 May 1903.
**** Originally named Wymondham until 1 September 1848, then Whisendine late Wymondham until 1 October 1878 and then Whissendine late Wymondham until 1 May 1891.
***** Originally named Manton for Uppingham until 1 October 1934.

Brookesby Station.

Saxby Station.

Manton – Kettering *

Original owning company	Midland Railway

Stations closed	Date of closure
Manton **	6 June 1966

* Closed stations on this line that were in Northamptonshire were Harringworth, Gretton, Corby and Geddington. From the late 1960s passenger traffic was diverted away from this line but in 2015 a limited through service between Leicester and St Pancras was reinstated.
** Originally named Manton for Uppingham until 1 October 1934.

Trent – Market Harborough (Midland Main Line) *

Original owning company	Midland Railway

Stations closed	Date of closure
Hathern	1 January 1960
Barrow on Soar & Quorn **	4 March 1968
Sileby ***	4 March 1968
Syston ***	4 March 1968
Humberstone Road	4 March 1968
Wigston Magna ****	1 January 1968
Great Glen *****	18 June 1951
Kibworth	1 January 1968
East Langton	1 January 1968

* Closed stations on this line that were in Nottinghamshire were Trent and Kegworth.
** Originally named Barrow until 1 May 1871 and then Barrow-on-Soar until 1 July 1899.
*** Reopened as new stations on 28 May 1994.
**** Originally named Wigston until 2 June 1924.
***** Originally named Glen until 18 January 1897.
      Originally named Langton until 1 May 1891.

Barrow-on-Soar & Quorn Station.

Barrow-on-Soar & Quorn Station.

Syston Station, *c.* **1900.**

Trent – Market Harborough (Midland Main Line)

Humberstone Road, November 1965.

Wigston Magna Station, 1952.